Books by *Richard Howard*

Poetry

FINDINGS   *1971*

UNTITLED SUBJECTS   *1969*

THE DAMAGES   *1967*

QUANTITIES   *1962*

Critical

ALONE WITH AMERICA   *1969*

Findings

For Helen
love
R...
'71

FINDINGS

Poems by Richard Howard

New York Atheneum 1971

The poems have been previously published as follows:

HARPER'S MAGAZINE (*The Chalk Cliffs of Rügen*)
IOWA REVIEW (*Recipe For an Ocean; Backing Down*)
KENYON REVIEW (*Leopardi*)
MINNESOTA REVIEW (*From Tarragona, Materia Medica, We Teach Antiquing, Lapsus Linguae, Demonstration*)
THE NEW YORKER (*From Beyoglu, Presenting a Watch*)
POETRY (*Giovanni da Fiesole, 209 Canal, Aubade, The Demolition*)
POETRY NORTHWEST (*Heart Failures*)
SHENANDOAH (*Beyond Words*)
TRIQUARTERLY (*Waiting for Ada, Prose for Borges, November, 1889*)

again, for Sanford Friedman

secundum artem

I

I I

(I)

From Tarragona

Dear Señor Parrilla (now I know,
    after an instructive shock
at the Alhambra-Palace, whose bar
    furbishes the neon fact
in lavender Moorish uncials:
    your name means grill-room! a fair
description, I should guess, of our times
    together, those thrice-weekly
sessions which closed upon a prospect
    of the alternative forms
taken by the imperfect subjunctive),
    Dear Arturo Grillroom, then,
a word—though merely indicative—
    for your efforts: *gramercy*,
that is my word, an archaic thanks
    to suit the sheer helplessness
of *any* language here, any term
    to match the time. Whatever
Spanish you managed to teach me stales
    as I sit here on the beach
before the town, watching it pour down
    the hill, motionless and still
perpetual. Even the oldest
    phrases of gratitude wilt
in this terrible light, this glower
    of centuries—hence my silence:
I speak to hold my tongue and my peace
    (it is the aporia
of the living muzzled by the dead)
    in the face of so much war
remembered or at least remodelled:
    La Cruz de los Caídos

elbowed aside by Roger de Lauria,
    Alphonso the Bellicose,
Jaime el Conquistador, even
    Saint Paul (who converted it
to Christ when upwards of a million
    souls could be saved in the town) —
statues rough with salt, green and ideal
    above me on the *Balcón*
del Mediterráneo. Above
    them, Catalan ruins prop
the Carlos Quinto donjon, and at noon,
    which is now, the *Copona,*
Archbishop Coponan's famous bell
    cast from melted Roman coins,
strikes in the cathedral (Romanesque,
    Gothic, then Lanceolate,
Flamboyant, Plateresque, finally
    Churrigueresque) built on the site
of a Mosque where the Temple of Jove
    once stood. Augustus lived here,
I see his sceptre's shadow falling
    over the Judería
renowned for doctors and bookbinders
    (some sixteen thousand volumes
crowd the Casa Consistorial,
    all in four dark rooms upstairs).
What words, teacher, for the Pelasgic
    Enclosure, Cyclopean
walls beneath the Scipian fortress?
    I write to tell you there is
nothing to say, and no news from here.
    The sea washes up to my
American feet as I stare down
    the beach to the menhirs left
by the Long Men of Medol Quarry:
    Behind me, in the Museo

Diocesano, are rusty hooks
    now rotted from their wooden
handles—their owners had no houses,
    but lived in the cliff fissures.
Like me they had no . . . words? left nothing
    for history but middens
which contained red pottery, antlers
    used as picks, ox-blade shovels,
a few bushels of shells, the bones of
    wild boar and goat, of roe-deer,
fox and badger; of three kinds of birds
    and seven kinds of fishes.

Beyond Words

His last month was July, the Summerland
    he called it, when one son
(the older boy) had taken poison: then,
    quite suddenly, he died too.

    Look—through the crooked window
he could never open, between branches
    of an old sour-cherry tree
bright with fruit—orderly there on the desk,

letters from his old ally and foe,
    paperweighted in packets
by two Offenbach scores: *La Belle Hélène*
    beside *Orpheus in Hell.*

    "You know this inmost aim, this
arrogance of my nature," he confessed,
    "to produce out of myself
a whole theater, a repertory:

not works, but rather a literature."
    In a real sense the man died
of responsibility, the sustained
    pressure of remembering

what had long been dismembered—
Europe, the wide land. Deep secrets hide
in surfaces, he knew, where else
could they go? and the spells we desecrate

run from mouth to mouth, unguessed, exhausted.
He fell, then, the Conjuror,
and all the puppets with him into whose
sawdust he poured so much blood.

Speechless they lay where he lay,
corpses who once had proved that what lovers
or friends mean to each other
is made clear by exchanging magic rings,

the presentation of a silver rose . . .
All gestures were ruined now:
the Madman's knee in Zerbinetta's eye,
Sophie with the awful nurse

hanging on her, Mandryka
sprawling, broken, obscene really, like them
all at this remove—merely
the others of *him*. That much of dying

could be rehearsed: for we are not ourselves
until we know how little
of our selves is truly our own. He knew,
now, how little and how much,

the Magician who leaped from
the father's into the son's body and
back, changing like clothes The Forms.
You can see the papers still, by this light,

though not the thread of script: it is too dark.
Branches move at the window
and bitter cherries like dead tanagers
brighten the grass where they lie,

shed the night before—droppings.
They sweeten, rot and dry. In an early
poem he said, "and yet, to say
'evening' is to say much." It is evening.

Giovanni Da Fiesole on the Sublime, or Fra Angelico's Last Judgment

for Adrienne Rich

How to behold what cannot be held?
Start from the center and from all that
lies or flies or merely rises left
of center. You may have noticed how
Hell, in these affairs, is on the right
invariably (though for an inside Judge,
of course, that would be the left. And we
are not inside.) I have no doctrine
intricate enough for Hell, which I leave
in its own right, where it will be left.

Right down the center, then, in two rows,
run nineteen black holes, their square lids off;
also one sarcophagus, up front.
Out of these has come the world; out of
that coffin, I guess, the Judge above
the world. Nor is my doctrine liable
to smooth itself out for the blue ease
of Heaven outlining one low hill
against the sky at the graveyard's end
like a woman's body—a hill like Eve.

Some of us stand, still, at the margin
of this cemetery, marvelling
that no more than a mortared pavement can

separate us from the Other Side
which numbers as many nuns and priests
(even Popes and Empresses!) as ours.
The rest, though, stirring to a music
that our startled blood remembers now,
embrace each other or the Angels
of this green place: the dancing begins.

We dance in a circle of bushes,
red and yellow roses, round a pool
of green water. There is one lily,
gold as a lantern in the dark grass,
and all the trees accompany us
with gestures of fruition. We stop!
The ring of bodies opens where a last
Angel, in scarlet, hands us on. Now
we go, we are leaving this garden
of colors and gowns. We walk into

a light falling upon us, falling
out of the great rose gate upon us,
light so thick we cannot trust our eyes
to walk into it so. We lift up
our hands then and walk into the light.
How to behold what cannot be held?
Make believe you hold it, no longer
lighting but light, and walk into that
gold success. The world must be its own
witness, we judge ourselves, raise your hands.

The Snake-swallower

He was quite a young man, and, judging from his face, there was nothing that could account for his having taken up so strange an occupation. He was very simple in his talk and manner. He readily confessed that the idea did not originate with him, and prided himself only on being the second to take it up. He said he saw nothing disgusting in it and spoke of the snake in general as a reptile capable of affection, not unpleasant to the eye, and very cleanly in his habits.

MAYHEW's *London Labour & the London Poor* (1851)

The snakes I use are not so long
    As you'd expect for show.
I try to find them thick enough
    To make the going slow,
Not slick. And always hold a pair
    Aside: you never know.
I keep them warm in flannel rags
    Or straw, but even so
The winter shrivels them to string
    After the first snow.

Straight off, and I was just a boy
    Before I started in,
They tasted queer: sticky, tart
    But sweetish too, like tin
When you bite on a knife. They draw
    The edge of your tongue thin,
And the roof of your mouth comes over rough

When the slippery skin
Slides. It helps to get there first
With a finger of gin.

The scales may scratch your pipe a bit
(Not so it gets scarred)
When you pull him back again.
A snake, see, moving toward
Ever so small a hole is like
Water being poured:
Smooth all the one way. Mind,
Don't show him you're scared,
Else he'll turn to a proper gag,
Stiff as any sword.

The head goes down about an inch
And the rest of him all
Continues in the mouth, curled round.
I hold him by the tail
And when I pinch, he goes in smart.
If you let him, he'd sail
Right down; mostly, though, they stop
After a two-inch crawl
Down the swallow; then they bind
In the mouth like a ball.

I was only the second that did it
Ever. The first you know
As well as me: our First Mother on
A night off, that's true.
It's nothing to do with what you like,
It's what you're used to:
I know a man bites the heads off
Chickens for *his* brew.
It isn't much different, what I do,
Except it's what I do.

Eve now, like I say, when she
  Took to the habit
Of swallowing, the country round
  Came quick to love it,
And don't they say, besides, somewhere
  That Christ came of it?
These days in the country, though,
  When you do it clever,
They swear you're the Devil Himself,
  And they won't have it.

The Chalk Cliffs of Rügen

for Robert Rosenblum

*Every authentic work is conceived
in a sacred moment, created in a
blessed one . . . The painter must
present not only what he sees before
him, but what he sees within. Other-
wise his pictures will resemble
screens behind which may be found
only invalids or even corpses.*
CASPAR-DAVID FRIEDRICH

This is the largest Prussian island,
   on which we have spent the day:
Ottilie and Walther, and of course Franz.
   There are ferry connections at Bug,
      should we desire to return,
and at Binz across the Baltic, were it
   opportune to extend an outing
      into a real excursion.
Rügen, a stronghold of Germanic tribes
   (the Rugii), fell to the Slavs or Scyths
      of old, and as recently
as last summer, when our Grand Duke came here
   for the first Goethe-Jubilaeum
      Picknick and Recitation,
bits of bronze would wash up the tide-strewn shore,
   where the dishevelled seaweed dyes the sea.
      "Bits indeed," Walther explained,
"vestiges of a horse-culture which carved
   its bridles with combat-signs." To which
      the Duke replied that the place
was rather like Paestum without the temples,
   the beach as passive as any stone
      inured to wine-libations,

and that such beauties imparted to it
  an amenity and an elegance
    hardly to be found elsewhere.
Franz, forever jealous of his spiritual
  attachments, as of his spiritual
    liberties, muttered he found
no inhabitants here but time, ever
  demolishing in silence. The phrase,
    one recalls, is Marmontel's.
No matter. Walther, a true lawyer, resumed,
  ever illustrating the obvious,
    explaining the evident.
And the Grand Duke generally uttered
  no more than "Ha," his convenient
    suspensive expression, or
laughed as if laughter could kill and he knew it,
  thinking of an enemy. Whereas
    Franz—three days out of the week
Franz is absurd, three days mediocre,
  and one day sublime. So much for that.
    We are not at Bug now, but above
the pale cliffs at Putbus; before us lie
  the sacred spaces of the sea, fields
    of light without a focus,
and to conceive our enchantment, you must
  imagine to yourself how a pearl
    might appear in a burning-glass . . .
That is the Hidensee, as it is called,
  wrinkling beyond the turreted V
    of chalk cliffs plunging from high
above us to far below. Already, Franz
  rejoices at having this time reached
    our perch without the Grand Duke,
whose liaison with Frau Korn, he grumbles,
  is no more than a macabre copy
    of Lord Byron's career but

conducted with one woman, on a less grand
  level, and in slower motion. One
    thing about Franz, evident
as he stands, bare-headed, staring out to sea:
  his Organ of Destructiveness is large,
    the Combative Lobe pronounced.
Ottilie clings to an alder-stump, pointing
  down to where the orifice widens
    in thunders of white silence
against the singing sea. Franz had begged her
  to accept the cloth—a red casheen—
    for her new riding-habit
(Scarpelain swore it was the true Parisian
  gorge de pigeon so fashionable
    this season), but now the brute
will not so much as deign to glance across
  the gully to where she sits, merely
    folding his arms and squinting
against the sun. "Little islands are all
  large prisons," he announces, and when
    Ottilie pouts and assumes
(one lovelock carefully loosened) what she calls
  a Récamier attitude, Franz inveighs
    against David: "Loathsome work—
he seems to have formed his mind from three sources:
  the scaffold, the sick-room, the brothel—
    it is all so laborious,"
he declares, "so tasteless—" "—but plausible,"
  Walther puts in, "his foliage being
    of the Single Leaf, and that
chiefly laurel, grape and bell-vine." "Devil
  take ten-thousand of them!" Franz will have
    nothing neo-classic: "Let us hear
earth's voices as they are, and the water's
  lovely dishabille—I would see *that!*"
    Ottilie shifts her pose, and

staring past the white ramparts to the sea,
   calmly remarks, "I shall live always
      —that is for me; I am living
here, at Rügen, eighteen-hundred twenty
   —that is for you. All is given us,
      Herr Fuessli says, and we have
nothing to ask for." Walther is kneeling
   now, at the brink, parting the grass-stems:
      who can tell if he follows
Ottilie's finger down where the cliffs fall,
   weightless, to the surf, or merely hunts
      for more relics in the turf?
Why has he cast away his his hat and stick?
   For answer he merely murmurs on
      in that absent drone of his,
"It is no naive illusion which makes men,
   and you too, my dear, seek eternal
      life. A limited future
makes our past unbearable. Nothing consoles,
   for nothing replaces . . ."
               There are two boats
   on the Hiddensee. The sun,
hewing the cliffs, is mighty now. Perhaps
   we have discovered what their shape, sharp
      against the water beyond,
reminds us of: it is a womb, a birth,
   a spanning of the earth no longer
      just a grave, delivering
Ottilie splayed against her alder-stump,
   and Walther sprawled at the verge, and Franz
      under his birch. So we are
born, each alone, in chaos while that waiting
   silence glows.
            And you will never know
   which of us has told you this.

Waiting for Ada

for V. Sirin

There is always another, one more,
one *last* Grand Hotel: far-fetched, far-flung,
but built to last. At least penultimate, surely,
Rimini's Grand Hotel du Miroir
stares down its methodical rivals,
modest interlopers on the English Parade
where all the pretty kiosks pointed
once as a matter of course to this
thermal term, this nearly pearly, nougat-textured,
art-nouveau pavilion readied now,
renewed this rainy April, for what
will never again be more than an off-Season.

Inside, I edge past the furniture,
oppressed by giant boudoirs no one
ever sulked in, knowing you would be at home here
—Hotel du Miroir! what better place?—
working wickedly away, when all
I can manage is to scavenge the lounge for books
and read till the rain relents: albums
of sepia views, and a German guide
to what our Air Force left of Malatesta's will—
these cannot beguile a mind obsessed
by what they bear eye-witness to: life
as it merely passes is so much time wasted.

And time saved? In store for me, once home,
your ardors loom, unspeakable loves
which ransom not by being beautiful or true
but by liberating us from *this*—

panoramas and preconceptions,
the places and the past we cannot recover
or truly possess save in the form
we give them. I leave all Grand Hotels
to you; the fishy photos slide away, the guide
to Rimini lies: Nothing exists,
and Never has existed always.
The rain stops. The Adriatic glows. Ada, I come!

209 Canal

Not hell but a street, not
Death but a fruit-stand, not
Devils just hungry devils
Simply standing around the stoops, the stoops.

We find our way, wind up
The night, wound uppermost,
In four suits, a funny pack
From which to pick ourselves a card, any card:

Clubs for beating up, spades
For hard labor, diamonds
For buying up rough diamonds,
And hearts, face-up, face-down, for facing hearts.

Dummies in a rum game
We count the tricks that count
Waiting hours for the dim bar
Like a mouth to open wider After Hours.

Leopardi

The palace at Recanati, crowned with merlons
and adorned with a bronze clock
boasts the remains of a Palladian fountain.
The piano nobile
houses a library of twelve thousand volumes.
One room is dedicated
to the poet (manuscripts, souvenirs, a marble
bust) who was born and lived here.

I   The locusts (we call them *cavallette*,
     little mares) that persist in singing
     after sunset are the ones will die
     next day. It is dark already. Who
     would believe how loud! I am trying
     to learn, from their voices, the dying fall.

II   I was in the garden, near the caretaker's house,
     sitting on a bench where the tired fountain drips;
     no one could see me there, for I had thrown a cloak
     over my shirt, and my face is not a pale one.

     Two young men lay on the steps, joking together
     under the colored lantern, drinking from a jug.
     How dark it was, between them and my hiding-place!
     And the first firefly—oh, bright as any candle.

     One of the two got up. I knew what would happen,
     prayed for mercy, implored the creature to fly off,
     but *he* clapped it out and strutted back to his friend.
     Just then Laura, our coachman's daughter, leaning out.

     of the window, plate and towel still in her hands,
     called back to someone inside: "What a night!
            can't see

your hand in front of your face." A moment later
the light in the window was put out. My firefly

had come to life again, and I prayed, etc.
but he noticed it, came swearing and knocked it down,
then stamped. His foot left a shining smear in the dust.
The garden filled with laughter. The jug was empty.

I heard a woman's voice I did not know: "Aldo,
it's late! Come to bed." More laughter, and some-
    one said,
"Here's the rain now." And I felt the light spring rain.
They all went in. I heard doors closing, and the locks.

III   There is no sleeping here in June.
Luckily they last only a night, the *cavallette*,
curse them!
then they too are done.

From Beyoglu

Dear Anne, counting here and now I can discover
    ten boats, no—a dozen boats.
  In this light or lack of it, in this
unlikely emptiness of air that lets me look
    miles up the Bosporus, miles
    down the Marmara to Kadiköy,
miles across the Horn to Usküdar, some dozen
    boats—lighted, each one, if not
  by light revealed—are set like moving
jewels in the water, shiftless, still; or perhaps
    it is the sky they're set in,
    plying up where further jewels fly
from Yesilköy to Ankara and all points East;
    the last few minutes lost me
  the horizon—there is no telling.

Before, when there was—say an hour ago, at least—
    a door in the minaret
  level with our balcony opened
and out stepped a man in shirtsleeves cupping both hands
    round his mouth. Whereat the air
  rang with calls to prayer, who could believe
how loud? There are little rings of light bulbs now
    just where that muezzin vanished
  once he'd bawled the sunset out of sight,
and all the world that is not Turkish—Turquoise!—turns
    ultramarine. Every light
  is a jewel, like the twelve boats—
even this balcony (to them) another gem,
    jewels the kind you love, Anne,
  the kind we saw in the Seraglio:

Amber drops labelled Tears of the latest Phoenix;
    Draconites engendered
  in the colorless brain of serpents;
an Amethyst whose liquor, at night, thickens to
    Sapphires which will melt the wax
  they're sealed with, even by moonlight;
cloudy Emeralds glistening in a glass as though
    slaves had licked them into shape:
  stones, jewels, lights! only farther off,
these, mocking sea, sky and the now invisible
    promontories. Atmosphere,
  in Istanbul, mimics History—
changing the sky, chaining the sea, leaching out all
    local color from the land,
  leaving dust and ash: the moon at noon.

This afternoon, our third, was a disaster here.
    Anne my dear, everything
  here is a disaster: closed, under
restoration, bricked up, broken, sadly lacking,
    reconstructed, brought down, now
  in disuse, utterly gutted, quite
ruined, badly weathered, reinforced, past repair,
    toppled, razed, formerly vast,
  slashed, scarred, contaminated, stripped,
stolen, sacked, defaced, vandalized, once resplendent,
    damaged by earthquake, lost, burnt,
  interrupted by the Sultan's death,
unexcavated, filled in, whereabouts unknown—
    we returned, without a word,
  to the hotel, twilight, and the view.

But at night these ashes glow, this dust kindles; like
    the Sultan's topaz, sallow
  then suddenly red, the moon turns Greek
fire, catches. While I watch I *hear* the past appear:
    the moment the moon rises

or the city, on its pyre, sinks back
to Constantinople, then to Byzantium,
    S in the room behind me
switches on the radio, full blast,
and a music fierce as the muezzin's fills the air—
    Finlandia. Dearest Anne,
    do you remember the year we were
Vikings? Monday after Monday, Miss Petersen
    started off with *The Silver*
    Songbook, Sibelius, 'O land of lakes

and azure streams a-flowing.' Sure, von Karajan
    conveys it better, the true
    Viking from Vienna. But the truth?
The trouble is I can't tell, Anne, can't tell the truth
    from travesty: children
    shrilling Sibelius in a ring,
supposing the black Finns to be their blond Vikings—
    we were those children, we sang,
    we suffered, we were there. Where were we?
Wasn't it real, is only *this* real: the complacent
    'stirring' orchestration here
    and now, and the moon, and Istanbul?
Are all those mornings' silver singing gone, when you
    and I were Great Lakes Vikings?
    They come upon me, and I am theirs.

Such music summons me to my own devotions,
    imperative as any
    howls from the minaret. How to find
a place for the past once it turns on you, and how
    to believe the present play
    of lights and placid sea? My dozen boats
have left the harbor basin black, till one ferry
    edges out from Galata,
    from the bridge they break in two at midnight,
and as it trusts itself to darkness, my answer comes—

25

nor is it, you would prompt me
from the songbook, as if we ever
lacked masters in displacement: Vladimir, Marcel!
There is another world—in
this one; the past is in the present

or nowhere. Mostly that, I find, in Istanbul:
a nowhere city faint
beyond finding, a site for Baudelaire,
"hospital whorehouse prison purgatory hell"—
until the moon turns it on
with a sound like Sibelius, grace
beyond argument or need granting the vision.
Unsounded, true Istanbul
contains itself in glory, all trash.
'The year we were Vikings' is here with the Blue Mosque,
a dim splendor depending
on a light, a sound, a memory
given, not gained. *Nothing is left, but nothing leaves:*
that is the Holy Wisdom
masquerading in Turkish Delight.

Even *Finlandia* comes to an end, but with it
comes a kind of solace, Anne,
a final comfort: the Finns are Turks!
Mongol types who share a language—Ural-Altaic—
'characterized by vowel
harmony, agglutinative forms
and uniformity.' Which sounds like poetry,
even like a poem, no?
once we know Sibelius was born
in Turku, Finland. S turns out the light, our room
ceases to be a jewel;
the ferry from Galata misses
Seraglio Point. It is dinner-time. Love, Anne dear,
from the European Side,
from Beyoglu, where I am. *Richard.*

Long Lines

for Lee Krasner

By night the day survives by night, outlasts its end,
Becomes what cannot be broken; for day in dreams
Is no longer day but dream, incessant language,
                    Interminable light.
We sleep, we dream: a constant allusion, a kind
Of perilous appeal, by the persistence of
What cannot end, to whatever bulks and bulges
                    Behind the beginning.
We sleep, we dream, we summon up the person—no,
The Being—of that first time, not the child only
But beyond the child, further, some vague myth: we dream
                    The void that came before.
The dreamer sleeps, but already knows in his dream
He is not the sleeper, is no one who can say
I am dreaming. For this is the realm, the region
                    Where pure resemblance reigns.
Here all is seeming, each figure the figure of
Another. Waking, we look for the model, seek
Originals. We want to be sent back, referred
                    To a point of departure,
The outset, an initial revelation, but
There is none. Our dream is semblance and returns us
To semblance, like unto like. There is no one here,
                    There is the dream, endless

Archiv. Mediceano 22.492 xliv

for Edmund White

They keep here in Venice, my lord, a Dragon
    Conveyed from Arabia, crossing
Sea and land in a great cage, living unharmed,
    Whereof I have taken the likeness
For that Perseus we did frame in your bath:
    It is of black lustre, the belly
Somewhat green, and most beautiful to behold,
    Boasting a treble row of white teeth
And clear-seeing eyes withal. Also it has
    Two dewlaps growing under the chin,
Hanging down like a beard, of a red color.
    The body is set all over with
Very sharp scales, and above the eyes as well
    To form a sort of leathern eye-lid.
The mouth (or so it is, my lord, in this most
    Tameable of Dragons) is but small,
Not bigger by much than a pipe, and through this
    It draws breath, yet wounds not with its mouth
But with the tail, beating about when angry.
    Since I arrived in Venice, my lord,
I have learned a new thing which will serve the work
    Even as the figure (now secured)
Of the Dragon. They have discovered to me
    A process of using powdered gold
Like any other color, and already
    I have designed anew the raiment
To show, in its oppression, a great glory
    Never seen in draperies before.
Shall we have Andromeda in a simple
    Gown or in a gold cloak of this guise

(As I should like her to be)? The rest I know—
    The procession following after
The rescue, led by Fame, upon whose mantle
    I have devised a thousand uses
For the dust of gold. And then are there not to be
    Four elephants drawing the chariot?
Yet advise, my lord, if you would have young men
    And fair maidens only in her train,
Or also famous old men? But yesterday,
    With the red hooded cloaks and a gown
For under it, bounty you have sent knowing
    The air of Venice ever unsure,
I had a letter from your Magnificence,
    Whereby (I understand) you believe
The Seraphims I made before setting out
    Upon this journey are out of place.
My lord, I have made but one, in a corner,
    Among certain clouds. Nothing there is
To be seen saving the tips of his bright wings,
    And he is so well hidden, so masked
By vapors that he does not at all advance
    The deformity of Religion,
But rather, in secret opposition to
    The Dragon, a studious beauty.
I have made another such on the facing
    Side of the bath, just where the water
Is let into the chamber, but also hid
    In a like way. Martigli has seen
And reported of them that there is no cause
    For displeasure, nor any echo
Of Devotion in all the embellishment.
    Nevertheless, as you decide,
My lord, once I am returned from Venetia,
    Two little cloudlets will take them off,
And thereto shall I contrive yet greater use
    For the new tincture, ever mounting

In a smoke of splendor from the Dragon's nose
    To cover all Heaven with the gold.
Is it not properly shown? My lord, I am
    Your servant, as I shall be always . . .

Prose for Borges

PROSE: *a poem so called because not in any regular meter, introduced on a special occasion and recited after others, hence also called a* SEQUENCE.

The cancellings, the negations are never
   ultimate, are never one last wipe
      that clears the lens, a farewell
to supersession, finale of ruin.

Is it because spirit is not strong enough
   to forgive flesh? The pardon that comes
      must come (if it comes) because
flesh forgives spirit. That is the work of prose:

to pardon, to perish. In other words—and
   prose is always other words—to be
      understood. Even pausing
in passing, the utterance must persevere

in its dismantlement, the vagabond turn
   moribund, till what had sought in us
      to assume a face, though one
of fragments, is discountenanced, disfigured.

Page after page, the old man goes on with it,
   making way for the everlasting
      Next, which exerts its power
by withholding its presence. Goes on with it,

his diabolic labor, to leave nothing
   fixed in the mind, obliterating

one damned thing after the next—
all the same, all damned. For what matters to us,

the only equality that matters, and
the only one we can manage, is
an equality in hell.
Yet ever and again, especially now

when the darkness closes in for good, closes
out the likelihood of replacements,
the impulse comes upon him,
the afflatus of unflinching. The old man

remembers a promise made by a parent
before speech, a premise enduring
the indignities of change:
what if the things which came out of time

and were changed could be made over, made over
so as to be thought of without time?
A language not out to
eliminate itself, resolute rather

to make a stay, creating the boundaries
it strikes against! That would be the speech
of angels. The old man smiles
at angels. Time and again he will try it,

the speech that stands against the spirit that moves.
But he is not an angel, the names
he listens for are the ones
omitted, rejected, unnamed. The old man

returns (a passion imitating an action)
to failure, to the new occasion

for failure, faithful to failure.
The task of his mind is never to begin

and never to end in the moment. Success
   repudiates the words it does not
     use. The old man uses up
what comes to mind. He repudiates nothing

except nothing. There is always more to be
   used up, to cancel, to erase. And more
     to perish. More prose. Because
there is the world, and because the world is prose.

November, 1889

for Harold Bloom

Well met, children! yet *I* am not well.
In their corruption, dear Fanny, all things are
    possible, none without. I thought so
today, riding on the water here to you,
            ill as I am, but not
            so ill as not to think,
        and with my burden besides—
        as blessings are a burden.
Has your man brought in
a bolted box, safe
        from the gondola? The burden
        I must give into your hands . . .
            Do I express myself,
            or but exploit myself?
        Astonishing, Pen, what you have done,
and managed yet to leave undone! Ruin at bay,
    procrastinated, nay proannuated!
Ca' Rezzonico and its eternal glooms,
            but not eternal now.
            We use the word amiss,
        as if it meant no more than
        "everlasting". Well! each bird
Sings to itself, so
then shall I, and make
        no more of your palace than
        that you have not made it less:
            here is a pile at last
            enabled to assume
        the full aspect of the past, which is
in Venice the period taken, or given,

34

for crystallization. I had thought
these walls beyond repair, like all such
            castles of misconduct,
            victims of villainous
        improvements else, reduced
        or even enlarged to being
one further orifice
in the peep-show here,
        lurid, livid, but always
        burnt out. It is easier,
            Venice and I have learnt,
            to endure than to change—
    hardest of all to endure what you
have not changed into. The bolted box is. . . but
    I shall explain. I am not very well.
Last week at Mrs Bronson's, it was no more
            than a migraine, or so
            the doctor in Asolo
        pronounced it—splendid fellow,
        what I liked most in him was,
he did not leave me
verses of his own.
        Curious symptoms withal
        for migraine: patterns moving
            over surfaces, faint
            most often, fine designs
    that would come as a kind of cobweb
cast iridescent upon others, a net
    intervening between me and them.
Lord! the things one sees when a fever-lit mind
            grants no middle distance.
            Prolixity of the real!
        And just when we are grateful
        for the dark, when night resumes us,
comes prolixity
of what is unreal,

the melting waxworks of our sleep
called dreams. I am against dreams,
not being one to trust
memory to itself.
In my delirium, then, I had
conviction of divided identity,
never ceasing to be two persons who
ever thwarted and opposed one another.
Then wakened to the faint
smell of drugs and nostrums
from the bedside—like a new-made
mummy. And as if in answer,
the post at Padua
(last month's, to be sure)
announcing Collins is gone.
Collins, Pen—Wilkie Collins,
the *Moonstone* man, although
fits and starts are the best
of what he left us: perhaps their length
is his measure. Well, we are all stewing-pans,
and can cook only what we can hold.
Some more than others. Collins had, poor fellow,
finicking manners but
a luxurious gut,
and he took his way sadly,
certain he had fallen among
grocers. A kind of
indispensable
liability to life,
that man's power of suspense;
and his tenacity!
One only does not call
a labor like *The Woman in White*
Herculean because Hercules could not
have done it! Whereas your father runs
after interruptions, leading or led by

the intransitive life
of a fool who foments
his poems whilst he dines out
and disappoints. Consider:
the torment of starch
in my new shirts, Fan,
has made me physically
irritable, morally
impotent, and *for days!*
Who could write, with a sense
of chalky grit rubbed into each pore,
clogging all perspiration, chafing every
inch of cuticle, desiccating
the blood itself! I share Gautier's opinion
that Christianity
and laundry cannot sort
together. Perhaps it was
Christianity and sculpture.
In either case, for
laundry *and* sculpture,
we should have one leg firm on
the Acropolis, and one
in Florence, For God's sake!
what organ have we then,
my boy, in Venice? If Asolo
be my *pied-à-terre*, here you keep, I suppose,
your *ventre-à-l'eau*. Monstrous levity,
to mask a lack. Shelley calls the great god Pan
a want, you know, and all
this Italian earth seems
now to me the sense of what
can never be. It burgeons
without us, and lives
the lewd life of things
that look for no existence
but in themselves. The canal

I came by—leave it and
it comprehends you not.
Worse, the admiration of mountains,
surely a Calvinist plot: strange confusion,
among minds defiant of meaning,
between the mere lofty and the beautiful.
If mountains turn a tree
into a fir, fancy
what they can do with a man!
Italy lets us know it:
the life of April
sunlight has to die;
it is now quite dead, and I
have another kind of life.
Beauties there, of course, but
coming only in bursts,
coming to a mind long crumpled (till
the creases stay), coming only in escapes
from the thing itself! Take Asolo,
that long Virgilian country round about—
half mystery and half
morality, but then!
then the scramble of rural
royalty, with royal thoughts!
"It is, at bottom,
would you not say, sir,
a criticism of life?" I:
"Rather take it at the top,
burning ever upward
to its blank point of bliss."
Sumptuous, of course, the dinner,
views from the villa entrancing, as you know:
the valley full of mist and looking
like a sea of absinthe, distant hills rising
from it, forming the shore
of Purgatory, past

Acheron. And the Russian
Duchess looked on indifferent,
staring as she ate,
watching the Brenta
     as if she were but watching
     the Grand Duke's body pass by:
          "What is there, that you make
          so much of, in water?"—
     leaving off the lobster—"I am quite
tired of it. There it goes: flow flow flow, always
     the same." She demands to see me here,
a Princess by birth, a Nihilist by trade!
          offers a rendez-vous,
          my dears, at her hotel,
     that I may explain stanzas
     she found *obscure*. I suppose
it is dangerous,
if you have not had
     the advantage of dying,
     to attempt a description
          of death, and afterwards
          there are, unfortunately,
     obstacles in the way . . . though Ba came
not to believe in those either. It is all
     rigmarole and rhodomontade, even
at the hands of a Grand Duchess practicing
          mesmerism and miracles
          on all sides. I sink to
     precious trifling, yet better
     than the fate of a fallen
rocket that likely
will be mine as well.
     I neither hope nor deserve
     to be loved by anybody,
          nor much, nor at all, yet
          I am very grateful

when someone is at pains to do it.
A great many such ladies of the first rank
were present at that dinner, and if
honeyed words from pretty lips could surfeit,
I had enough—though one
can swallow quantities
of whipped cream and do no harm
to an old stomach. They seem
to care so deeply
for what they call *art:*
I suppose it is like one
of those indelicate subjects
which always sound better
in a foreign language.
I am not interested in art.
I am interested in the obstacles
to art. One creature with queenly airs
and a snake, I vow, tattooed on her ankle,
clung to me like ivy:
whatever should she do
in order to become, say,
a poet? *In order!* Never
have I pretended
to afford anyone
such literature as might
substitute for a cigar,
but so much I told her:
"Don't twitter, though sparrows
all do; things happen, and then we get
a lark or a nightingale or even an owl,
which last is by no means to be scorned."
Kay Bronson cannot abide, you know, the rule
of an equal number
in men and women guests.
She says she invites her friends
for conversation, not mating.

Even so, there are
surprises. Walking
    in the woods with my snake-lady,
    I said: "Let us sit here"; then,
        after regarding me
        steadily a moment,
    her pale eyes glowing like grapes,
she said: "You may make love to me, if you like."
   The old have death, and the young have love,
but death comes once—love over and over.
        Or is it to the old
        that death comes back and back.
    and love no longer at all?
    I told her, it was for poetry
I ate and drank and
dressed and had my being,
    but she would not let me go.
    To be quit of her and them
        is a godsend to me,
        for all the graying wreck
of nature here, where if not divine
it is diabolic. I said I was not well,
    yet well or ill, up at the villa
I am a man smothered with society
        of women, like a duck
        with onions. I will not
    be Victorian in their way:
    I would be . . . Albertian!

In the one year, Ba
died, then Albert died.
    Ours were the Great Marriages,
    I cannot help but think, for
        I know ours to be, still,
        the Great Bereavements,
    the weeds worn so long neither the Queen

nor I remembers quite the flowers, I daresay,
   sprouted by now to something emblematic,
something gone out of the garden altogether.
        Wife to husband, widow
        to widower, ah, Pen,
     we remember the flowers,
      in thirty years forget the weeds!
I want nothing left
out, and nothing back,
     no, nothing ever again.
     Don't expurgate: exorcise
        your losses! In Venice
        we learn about losses:
    they affect us only till we have
lost altogether. Then comes a poisonous
   impalpability that simulates
a form beneath the flow of time's gray garment,
        and through the place we see
        is signified a place
     we never saw. Life is all
     salutation. No reply.
Drifting through Venice
after twenty years'
     such drifting, and year by year
     seeing only the bruises
        in the marble blacker,
        the patience of ruin
    deeper, every stone an image of
accumulated sea-change, it was all one—
   one of my numerous visions which so
numerously leave me. As I came, my box
        beside me and my eyes
        too old for disbelief,
     clouds soon covered up the sun,
     as if too good to be seen,
granting a dead glare,

visions from the verge
   shadowless in the steel air,
   unaccountable, violent
     against an ultimate
     horizon. At that hour
  the ends of the earth were closing in,
and I thought: my boy, my Pen, cold walls hold him
  among shades and silences, mostly
darkness there, under a grim incessant sky
     grayer with each moment
     since Asolo. It was
  a pale departure into
  this perfect decrepitude,
suffering this dim
disgrace of daylight
   as the noiseless town neared us.
   Neared *us!* We could not even
     creep to it, but Venice
     rose up out of the sea
  to meet us, a momentary shape
made magnificent by perennial touching.
  Ah, Fanny, there are times I can guess
what you good young Americans must feel, times—
     I feel them too—when we
     are nothing but the heirs
   or an humiliating
   splendor. As you have taught me,
it takes a great deal
to make one successful
   American, but to make
   one happy Venetian takes
     a mere handful of life
     among old stones. Indeed,
  if there be disagreeable things
in Venice, nothing is so disagreeable
  as the visitors, jostling for boats

    around one. Lady Gordon warned I should find
        a *bateau-mouche* plying
        the Grand Canal! I had
      no distaste for it, myself,
      but the gondoliers, finding
    their custom lessened,
    had all struck, and we
      could barely get a *barca*
      for love *as well as* money!
        Poor fellows, they shall learn,
        as others have, that steam
    is stronger than they. We left behind
   those foreigners fuming round the Redentore,
    and I knew: what is dead or dying
  is more readily apprehended by us
        than what is part of life.
        Nothing in writing is
     easier than to raise the dead.
     Do not let me wander, Pen—
I am not enough
myself now to be
      spontaneous. I must *scheme*.
     Last year, Eliot Norton
        (I have learnt to admire
        if not to endure him)
    showed me the letters to Jane Carlyle
and those from her to Thomas, before and since
    their marriage, both. He will not print them,
even to correct Froude's falsifications,
        will not violate *anew*
      the prostrate confidence
   of husband and wife, will not
    be known as the one to do it,
at any rate. Pen,
such must not be my fate.
     I dread but one thing: biography.

The truth which is in this box,
        once unlatched, once published
        to the world, is worth all
    the tragedy of errors after:
time finds a withered leaf in every laurel,
    age makes egoism more eager,
less enjoying. It shall be her words, my words,
        no more than that, no less.
        There are enough of them,
    five-hundred letters, by my count—
    long ago. What our words are,
I am not certain.
It is done. Old love
        is slow in going, but goes.
    Some twenty years since I looked
        at what is in the box.
        Cowardice, call it that;
    I do not know the name. Sufficient
for me, knowing they are there. Without opening,
    I can say the words, some of the words:
"My power lives in me like the fire in those mad
            Mediterranean
        phares I have watched at sea,
    wherein the light is ever
    turning in a dark gallery,
still bright and alive,
and only after
    a wary interval leaps out,
    for a moment, from the one
        mean chink, and then goes on
        with between it and you
    the blind wall." Perhaps because I can
recite that much, I do not care for the rest.
    You keep them now, Pen, and once I am
gone, give them to Smith. It should be two volumes . . .
        Nothing but ourselves then,

        though that be too much now
    for me. Put the box away,
    high and dry. I am still here.

Now this is splendid,
what you have done with
    the stairs, Fanny, this is warm!
    it shows what *can* be done. If,
      as I have always said,
      these people are ever
refined, it will be by fire. A few
coals do it: the life in us abolishes
    the death in things. I recall, last time,
how drear it all looked, and how I dreaded
      to feel the pale hush
      of the irreparable
    on all these blighted rooms,
    the relics of how many
Doges littering
your inhuman walls?
    A pressure of sanctity
    almost profane, disorder
      in the very daylight . . .
      All gone, now, and well gone
    behind us, or ahead—like the letters:
too far behind me to be endured, too far
    ahead to be dared. Let them rest here.
Ah, Venice! Pen, your Venice now, how it rocks
      all ambitions to sleep,
      floats a man to his doom,
    even when the secular truth
    is a stroll on the sandbars.
Again the delusion!
We are all under
    a net that covers the world!
    Or is it but the canal,

lapping in light on your
ceilings? It is nothing,
then, no cause for alarm, dear children,
it has passed, as all spells do, however cast.
The preponderance of some dissolving
force, mine or water's, need not be contended with,
merely endured, merely
survived. Strange, though, how close
the meshes were, everywhere
entrapping, overtaking . . .
If I am to go
out to the Lido
at all, I must go before
I am too sick to go, and
above all, before I mind
being sicker. Let me have
my cloak again, Fanny, and your man
to row me beyond these wicked walls. I want
to see the grass, if it be but gray
wires curling on the beach. I need to walk now,
without these palaces
pressing in upon me;
they make, for all their marble
pride, a valley of darkness—
at its end I see
vast uncertainty.
I want room now, not solace,
I must have the roar and release
of some open water,
even if it be black.
Then here, returning, then the firelight,
then, in the winter half of the world, to sleep . . .

(II)

Scenes from the Life of Behemoth

for W. S. Merwin

A Robin Redbreast in a Cage
Puts all Heaven in a Rage.   BLAKE

Under shady trees he lies, thus it is written,
And the willows of the brook compass him about.

> Differing, if we may trust the hand
> Of a Dürer, working by report,
> From all other beasts, saving the eyes,
> Which are like bears. For although there be
> Many that have the single horn, yet
> Is there none having that one to grow
> Out of his great nose but this alone,
> And harder than any teeth or bone.

The green branches cover him, spreading a comfort
On the wilderness of reeds and fen, wet places.

> Two girdles guard his body, they are like wings
> Of a dragon, coming from his back
> Down to his belly, which is colored
> Like bark or rind, whereupon there grow
> Hairs seeming somewhat red, and his flank
> Is distinguished with certain purple
> Hieroglyphs upon a golden ground,
> Fading toward the loins and hinder parts.

He is taken by the same means as the Unicorn:
For he cleaves to Virgins, be he ever so wild.

Oppian alleges in his book
There was never yet a distinction
Of sex, for all that ever were taken
Be males and not females. But from this
Let it not be gathered that there are
No females whatsoever alive,
For, reader, it were impossible
That the breed should continue without.

Above all other creatures does he love Virgins,
Thus it is written, and unto them will he come.

Fetched out of the Indies, he was shown
First in Holland, anatomized by steel
And brush. Albinus to Geo. Stubbs: "Sir,
If ever I was surprised, I was it,
Surely, by your painting of the Rino
Ceros. For you have given him out
In all the colors of Apocalypse,
Worthy of pursuit to Paris, even . . ."

And will fall asleep before such Virgins, and so
Being asleep, is easily carried away.

In a great gaol, drawn by twenty horse,
The monster (*videlicet*, a thing
Shown, de-monstrated) passed from Holland
Into Germany, where he was figured
Forth, and boldly, by the Swiss limner
Rüdinger. And by June of that year,
(Even as the great *Esprit des Lois*
Was licensed) he had come to Versailles.

A wonder in Nature, both for the outward shape,
And also for the inward courage and mildness.

Here, for one-hundred thousand écus,
Was he offered to the Menagery
Of Lewis Fifteen. "That is too much,"
The royal factor replied, and from
Oudry commissioned no more than two
Likenesses for the Blue Pavilion.
Besides, from much whetting on a stone,
The horn was clearly coming undone.

All that his horn is set to, either he casts up
Into the air, or bears through, though it be iron.

There is not only a discord, but
Some natural enmity between
This beast and the elephant, which may
Exceed him in eminence; for when
The Monoceros (with the horn loose)
Was at Lyons, and was brought into
Presence of an elephant, why then
The elephant ran away from him!

So strange an outside yields an answerable heart
And testimonies of virtue comprised within.

To Venice then he came, where Longhi
Portrayed his horrid splendor, the horn
Detached, passing through hands of ladies
Masked for Carnival, and one sequin
Now the price (which Casanova paid)
To see the beast entire, until taken
To Verona, shown there one last time
In the Roman amphitheater.

Only see his brute stature, and one cannot choose
But find matter rare and strange, unknown to the mind.

Now a girl tends him with her milch cows,
Mild as they are, and ignored by them.
The beast is dying, will die, this year
Of Gray's *Elegy*, first of his kind
In Europe, of which he has seen five
Nations beyond his Indian heath.
This grass is not the same, and the girl
May be no virgin, for he cannot sleep.

Behold now Behemoth. Thus it is written, where
Beasts of the field play, he eateth grass as an ox.

On Arrival

Waiting is the poem of waiting.
    Tomorrow you will be here
and I can leave off the anthology,
    heroic couplets, haiku,
projective verse—it is all making
    do, and it has done for me
whatever making can: a coming
    to terms with nothing, until
something is on those terms, my poems.
    By tomorrow this waiting
will be over and done with, it will
    be my best poem ever,
and it will never have been written.

Presenting a Watch

Here where help is another transaction,
    sleep something we *do*,
you must have discovered, my dear, we have
    a Dorian mode
of our own, Dorian Grave: we keep death
    out of our faces
by foisting it off on our wrists. So that
    while not much more than
the weather may seem to happen to us
    in our capital
of group therapy, there it is each time
    we light a cigar
or kiss someone: the mindless reminder
    that when we leave off
counting we can no longer live up to
    ourselves. We become
aware of the void only as we fill it,
    in other words, with
no words for the minutes except one: *more.*

Wonderful, is it not, that such a thing
    is called a *movement?*
From what? To what? The movement is between
    two evils, neither
the lesser. That is why it is called,
    also, an *escapement.*
I give you the time of day, give it away
    not because I wish
our companionable curse on you, not
    because I prefer
to rid your face of just what I found there,
    wanted, haunted, home—

but to share its minor music ticking
      on us both: the fear
of losing is what we possess, the hope
      of uniting all
that divides us. You will get the message
      once you wear this bright
engine as I wear mine, *in the meanwhile.*

Aubade

The window pales, and by its paltry light
    I lose you. I want more.
Rousing (if I ever slept) I slither
    Out of bed, cautiously
Holding my breath, and my breasts in both hands,
    Until the straw subsides
And with no more than a frown you resume
    Your peremptory snores.
We have made a hot night of it, one way
    Or another, and now

The shutters open onto a darkness
    Already not itself.
I'll close them, rescuing the universe,
    And return in the same
Silence, breathless with anticipation,
    To my place beside you,
Biding my time to take it, when I can,
    By some becoming move.
I watch your body wake and make in each
    Of its private partings

A circuitous gesture (I wonder
    Why they call it coming)
Hardening fast into departure.
    From memories of maps
You'd suppose it is the same avenue,
    A coming-to that must
Be come to once again, but believe me
    It is a new journey,
On these slopes you will take another fall
    Altogether, past old

Suspensions to the present standpoint for
    That final balancing
Act of darkness, while in the sudden
    Landscape, time—dear, time dies.
Nothing here will ever happen twice, no
    Two mouths drink from the same
Sluggish river, nor one flesh (which we are
    Made) be the same giver.
We trust too much to words, repeating mere
    Names that were meant for once.

I stare the disfigurements of your sleep
    Into countenance: up!
Odd what we take it into our heads
    To urge, and stop our heads
On a steep but merging syllable: O
    It is a gift of tongues
And lungs we lavish on your limbs, thirsting
    For the first occasion
To worship, in the articulate temple,
    The unspeakable god.

Backing Down

All right I'll unsay them ravel or
unravel my rows of neat stitches
rub out the whole drawing line by line
    until there is nothing
left of what I meant to say All right
I meant nothing in particular
and by undoing the general too
    until there is nothing
of that either which is just as well
when was the general any good
I'll erase even the blank spaces
    until there is nothing
where to all intents and purposes
there was nothing anyway All right
there was but I won't remember it
    until there is nothing
no intent no purpose and no good
perhaps when it is all gone All right
only then taken out of our hands
    until there is nothing
we may discover what comes instead
the god comes call it coming there are
no words All right no words the god comes
    because there is nothing.

Heart Failures

My dear, you described it
in such clear detail I should have seen
for myself, suspected from the start.
    You know how we are, though,
all of us (even yourself, surely?)
about these things: reality comes hard
    and never fast enough
to be the rule . . . I suppose the rain
distracted me, the storm in the air
    but not yet upon us.
Still, just your tone must have meant *something*
at that point—the really awful part
    when your father drove you
all those flat miles out to the new farm
(your voice faltered then), arriving there
    with the rain that came down
soon like dye, darkening everything.
You watched him run, hunched and determined
    between the black puddles
to an ominous haystack, and then
it happened, silent in the blurred lens
    of the Packard windshield:
as if he *meant* to, sliding slowly
into the mud. You had never heard
    of a coronary,
and when he cursed you back to the car
you obeyed, of course. What could you do
    but peer through the downpour
while his limbs twitched, and a kind of mist
—the emanation of pain, it was—
    aureoled his body
where it lay in the rain another

> hour until a neighbor took you both
> away. Remembering
> how you turned into a child again,
> just telling it, *his* witnessing child,
> I guess who I am, too
> (it was all so simple, once you set
> the scene), lying here awake, lying
> with what is left of you
> cold in the sheets against me. The rain
> hisses under traffic—it has come
> for good then, so to speak.
> I know who I am *for you*. I know,
> suffering my private spasm here,
> how anonymously
> you yielded when I caught your long legs
> in mine: not yours, not mine. From how far
> you must have been staring
> through what dim glass, while my foreign nerves
> performed! I know who I am—who cares?
> It is as true of this
> seizure as of that other: *having*
> teaches us little, nothing of love
> whose presence we locate,
> and whose power, only in our losses.
> You stir in my arms and say, "I thought
> the rain would never come."
> Now that it has, my dear, I almost
> fear that it will never end. Never.

The Difference

Looking at you
I cannot help surmising
As I admire the view
That a landscape so enticing
Must be also true.

Cast in their unwrinkled case,
The apportionment
Of featured precincts in your face
Surely represents
A genuine genius of the place.

But looking at me
I find it hard believing
Myself is what I see
—As if by merely moving
My face might get free

Of what is nothing more than some
Irrelevant mask.
On you it's you, and even dumb
Owns what I must ask:
Mine the foreign parts, yours home.

Death Sentences

Yours will begin over and
over, which is the only joy, beginning.
Mine keeps ending, a seism
in seity.

Yours is a mouth: what we become.
Mine an eye: what we are.

Something in the wind, yours
arrives out of the blue,
no natural cause but a consequence,
seeking the center.
Mine blooms, an escaping
flower.

Yours will come to you across
fields, over stones, and streams will sing
its approach.
Mine spreads outward, rises
to the surface, in silence.

You will own yours.
Mine is my tenant.

Spitting, yours will spit blood,
saliva, what there is to spit.
Mine, my tongue.

Yours can keep a secret, even from you.
Mine has none,
is one.

In other words yours will be other,
mine more of the same.
you will be me.
I will be nothing.

Materia Medica

for Dr. Robert Seely

When he heard
The news that night from Kimbolton,
The King dressed in yellow with a white
Feather in his cap, and gave a ball
At Greenwich, going ever about
Among the revellers with the Princess
In his arms and saying, "God be prais'd,
The old harridan is dead, now there is
   No fear of war further."
                Whereupon
Señor De la Sà, that was the Queen's
Doctor from Spain, opened the body
For embalming, being then alone
But for one other servant. He found
Every organ healthy save the heart
Which was all blacken'd and hideous
To see, with a black growth adhering.
   This was a mystery,
              And remains,
In the testimony of De la Sà,
Starred with the suspicion of poison.
So, the Queen dead, the King exulting
With the baby Princess Apparent
On his breast—such is the condition
Of the Realm, this Kingdom I serve too,
The self I inhabit like a Throne . . .
   For as I lay writhing
              On the floor,
My body my enemy (yet my own
Spies in the enemy's pay), at war

With the very processes that once
Had made me live, I was the beldame
With the black heart. And as you wrestled
—"Breath into *this* now! try not to move"—
With what I had ceased to own, merely
    Identifiable,
              No longer
An identity, I discovered
All the wisdom of the cast-off Queen:
"Let it be over, this must end!" Now
I wait for *your* discoveries, dressed
In an easy raiment like the King's,
Hugging my reft ego back to me
Like some royal heir; and reconstruct
    That solemn inquiry—
              A varlet
Holding the torch, the papery sound
Of skin, old skin, parting, and the tall
Shadows as the Spanish doctor cuts . . .
Doctors are forever dividing us
Into Infernal Parts, yet as soon
As the seizure breaks, we put the parts
Together: this body we gainsay
    And may be given back,
              More or less,
Is immortal. Only the mind dies,
Doctor, only the mind can kill us,
Waging a War of Succession on itself
In this disputed regency of ours,
Its forces mercenary, mobile, mean;
Only the mind in pain will believe
There is nothing, nothing but itself—
    Or what we call the mind,
              Deciding
Like the King that war is past because
The black-hearted Queen is gone, fond King

With the future in his arms, holding
War that grew even as it withered
Behind him in the Spanish bedclothes . . .
There is always the chance of poison,
Señor De la Sà allowed, peering
   Into the corpse by night,
               And we know
The heart nowadays for being black.
The King's himself again, the Princess
Crowing as he gloats, no looking back.
It is our selfhood that we know in them,
Doctor, our dynasty and our death,
Not to forget the discarded Queen:
Who Succeeds, we die to prove, *who fails*
   And who follows failure.

We Teach Antiquing, Distressing, Burning-in, Marbleizing, Gold-leafing, Tortoise-Shell, Glazing, Mottling, All Finishes

"Richard!" you cried, "redress me and release
the likely self lies locked within
these wards my surfaces:
refurbish—" this, mind, to one reputed
knowledgeable in varnishes,
"or at least refinish
edges that else will turn lunatic fringe
altogether!" Lord knows I stared
hard, startled that your limbs
allowed (as if they had a choice) right then
and there what seemed prohibited
to me all along: Ease,
the movements of a melt, and precisely
the enterprise of grace that gains,
so far as I can see,
your whole being when your body no more
than undertakes another mode
of rearranging air.
Look at it my way: even as I watch
the marvelous crib of muscle,
meat and bone creating
what you mourn as your immurement, to me
the very durance so deplored
by you must still *be* you:
the cage, as I see it, is the captive.
There, we are all alike. Even
such casual wrapping

as mine, reconciled though I may—must—be
to its now wrinkles, dissembles
a smooth ego inside
I despair of disporting. Apprentice,
here are your beakers and retorts,
the rude contrivances
whereby to work an alternative rind—
much good may they do you, or none,
though you make yourself free
with all my skill at superficies:
the very skin you undermine
is the one I mark out
for my own, cunning docent that I am
of dermae, scalps, integuments—
all the outside chances
O my dear, of coming in the first place.

Lapsus Linguae

*I do not believe anyone will make
mistakes in an audience with His
Majesty, in a declaration of love, or
before a jury.*

THE PSYCHOPATHOLOGY OF
EVERYDAY LIFE

What a relief, to find it in the *language*,
    at last; to realize, stunned,
as table after tableful of diners
    circled slowly in the filthy
din of El Faro, what it was: of course!
    we were at a *repast*, the name
for just that crisis of spirit when the world
    seems to have happened once before
already, when each word is made dubious
    by some distorting slur. You swayed,
swung back to me (the Scotch? the Spanish food
    too late at night?) and blurted out:
"Richard, I have these solitences, you know."
    I knew; in fact I welcomed them,
watching the scaffold of an identity
    collapse, watching the mind's thistle
scatter blown as by a breath, watching you
    drop a fork, knock over (twice)
my glass, lunge at the passive gold *paella*.
    Freud said that invariably
elements lying *outside* the intended speech
    account for our errors in it.
"Solitudes, I mean—no, silences . . .Well,
    both," and you smiled then so I
cannot forget how your eyes retreated deep
    into their caves (by that light,

deeper than ever) where I would follow them,
    though what would be the good? We make
no mistakes when we are *all there*, but always
    there is the past again, repast
of our absences. Slips of our mother tongue.

The Demolition

for Maurice Green

Of course there has to be a reason, doctor:
  I'm late because I was early, not
    on time to reach your office
      in time—that will come
  with time. Meanwhile, just to while away
    the time ahead, I lingered . . .

  No, officer, I'm not *loitering*
here, only looking, like these other people,
    at the wreckers while they work.

    We stood there staring,
      doctor, as the great steel ball
rummaged gently through what used to be
      your rooms—all those hours
collapsed so easily, just a touch does it—
    snapping off the pipes, twisting
girders, leaving (obscenely) the patch of green
    wall with the Edwardian molding
      I could make into a groin,
        sometimes, from the couch.

  Then the crane took it all, clearing out
the rubble in one or two bites, big ones though,
    and drooling the leftovers.

It was at that moment, doctor, as I watched,
  I knew for once, at once, what we have
    come to call, in our sessions,
      my resistances,

        the ligatures and liens on a life
        I could not gladly let go.

    There they were, still, and above them rose
slowly into the already littered air
        a cloud of white plaster dust.

        For all the ruptured
        tubes and ripped-out masonry,
    it was quite silent, actually
        tranquil as the last
laths went, and I turned away, late already
        for you, doctor, wondering
as I hurried to the new address, the clean
    partitions, if those waiting others
        were patients too, watching
            themselves come apart.

    Did you know, officer, that *loiter*
derives from *loutish*, from *lurk*, even from *lie?*
    Does that make it easier?

Hopkins said the mind has mountains, he was wrong:
    it has plumbing and plaster, parquet
        and marble shards like this one
            I am fingering;
    and such intestinal obstructions
        go up in a little smoke,

    witnessed by uneasy bystanders
waiting, like me, now that I am here at last,
        for the new sutures to be

        fastened, made fast
        among all this bright Finnish

furniture. Waiting, doctor, for that
    old visitation,
the unreconstructed self, to take revenge
    for a wrecked interior
decoration, a few flimsy walls knocked down
    which stand, yet no longer standing, for
        years of my mind where I could
        call myself my own.

Doctor, I'm afraid (that old ghost story)
I'm late. Sorry to have been malingering.
    We must begin all over . . .

Uncertainties of an Old Patient

Long ago, doctor, when I was a boy
    Or a girl, I forget which
It is so long ago, before these mean
    Days that have no sacred word,
I dreamed the dream of my father standing
    On a hill and speaking fair
To those of us in the field below, and
    Thereupon we saw appear
A circular flame which of a sudden
    Vanished away, and he fell.

No, that was not a dream, doctor. Was it
    Perhaps the next I recall
Which I meant to tell, a genuine dream
    This time, to the best of my
Recollection, a dream in which a red
    Stole keeps me from making out
A woman who stares over the landscape:
    I make a noise, I whimper
Maybe, and she turns, slowly turns round
    To face me—her face, doctor,

Is covered with scars and scaling bruises!
    She has fallen—I ask her
And she has fallen, she says, ascending
    A ruin. Was that a dream?
Doctor, I cannot tell my dreams. Cannot
    Decide what may have happened
And what is but hearsay or a hoped-for
    Vision. Here is the last dream
I remember, or the last memory dreamed.
    Help me, doctor, to resolve . . .

There came past me, then, a basketwork cart,
    Hooded, two-wheeled, the axles
Creaking, and in it a kind of Holy Man
    Yellow-skinned and bound about
With silk, yellow as well, who like an idol
    Sat rocking even as the cart
Was drawn past me by an ancient priestess
    Who kept heaping up around him
Melons and blue plums and great bruised pears
    And oranges. The cart passed

Then, and as I stood gaping after it
    The last thing I saw was that
Child, the body of a child hanging down,
    Head downward, bleeding and pale,
Not like those beautiful fruits, that perfect
    Flesh which filled the cart with juice,
But broken and dead, I think, depending
    From the axle of the cart.
They went on then, the yellow-swathed idol,
    The priestess, and the dead child.

That is the one dream I do remember
    Dreaming, it did not happen,
Did it? Of course it may be no more than
    Reality, it was long
Ago, so long. I was inspired then, I was
    Almost a poet, and you
Never discover who is an inspired
    Poet—I have learned that much
In all these years with you, doctor—
    Till the inspiration goes.

The Failure of Nerve: An Epoch

for Anthony Hecht

> ". . . *when her 24-year-old son died*
> *today, she permitted the Society to*
> *freeze his body. Asked if she would*
> *agree to her own body being frozen,*
> *for a possible resurrection, she re-*
> *plied, "I don't think I want another*
> *chance at this life."*
> *The New York Times, August 1968*

Meaning by "failure", I suppose, no more
    Than the success of many
Another thing, merely, as the weeds may
    Succeed and a garden fail:
Success of hope, then, and of the substance
    Of what is hoped for—the faith
We call imaginary because it is
    Impossible to imagine.

It is not my word, but my Mother's word.

Do? This you must do: replace what you are
    By what you know (remember,
You do not know what you are). It will take
    About six hours for the task,
But you must begin at the right moment.
    Watch the eyes, they will tell you
When to begin. Ignore the mouth, the hands.

It is not my act, but my Mother's act.

Of course the refrigeration process
    Will have started long before:

Drain off the blood, replacing pint by pint
    With glycerol, a saline
Solution of twenty per cent. Increase
    Refrigeration until
Transfer to the styrofoam cannister.

It is not my need, but my Mother's need.

Whence you will remove it to a final
    Repository, inside
A steel vacuum capsule ten feet long,
    Into which is pumped liquid
Nitrogen, lowering the interior
    Temperature to three hundred
Degrees below zero, Fahrenheit scale.

It is not my will, but my Mother's will.

Whereupon is no prospect of an end
    (The nitrogen, through a tube,
May be replenished at large intervals).
    The flesh does not turn to dust,
But remains, until the future may find
    A means to regenerate
The cells. The brain, naturally, is gone.

It is not my peace, but my Mother's peace.

The Greek says we are awake, all of us,
    In the same world, but we sleep
Each in his own. We sleep, let me tell you,
    Beneath the moon, without end.
The ultimate purpose, bear in mind, is
    The total defeat of death,
The triumph of a life to come after.

It is not my death, but my Mother's death.

We are beneath the moon. The sacred beasts
    Return, sable and silver
Like the night and the moon. With them the damp,
    The ills of earth, and the bad
Daemons. Above the moon, necessity
    Rules, chance not. We are beneath
The moon, and here we endure as we may
    That future past which is death.

It is not my life, but my Mother's life.

Recipe for an Ocean
in the absence of the sea

You have the ingredients on hand.
    Get to the edge of something,
    yourself best of all, and take
yourself in hand. Take, I mean, your hand,
    trace out the blue menaces
    released and lapsing there,
watch closely around the wrist: they will
    remind you what you must do.
    They are what you must do. Be
them, until there is nothing but them,
    then you are ready. Now take
    time, all there is in the house—
it does not have to be yours. Take time
    and never for a moment
    losing track of what changes
back into yourself, bitter enough
    so that you will need almost
    no salt, mix well and then leap
over the edge. Wait there. When you can
    wait no longer, it is done.
    Serve at once. It does not keep.

Demonstration

That day there was no telling
A gray sky from a grey sea:
      The horizon
A lie or no more than an imaginary line, at most
    The difference between two
    Vowels no one's hearing can
Discriminate. The sky looked a degree colder maybe
      Than that other
    Grey, but just as unbounded.
    No horizon, then, out there,

      .

    No end to the weather, but
    Endless beginnings, false starts
      From premises
Known to be unreliable, groundless, without a clue
    To what was coming or had
    Come already, Biddeford
Pool this August without sun, this Tuesday without a sign
      Of the time now,
    Though it had to be daytime—
    A day of no hours, no source

    For the unwavering light
    That glared across the water
      While three men rowed
Out to the place, or the hoped-for replacement of what seemed
    The place where they had lost (Here?
    Here?) a dozen lobster traps—
Biddeford Pool, then, a suburb of the sea, reflected
      The empty sky
    Only, as air echoed (Here?
    Here?) an equally empty

Ocean. There was no warning,
No warrant but the weird hunch
This would be where
Richard Gagne and his brothers might retrieve the missing
pots
(Here? here?) which must have drifted
Beyond all calculation
But the cast of chance. These fishermen trusted to their luck
Off the Saco
Breakwater, still within sight
Of land that lay behind them

And within the sound—closer—
Of the fog signal: here? here?
The siren kept
Asking them, never singing, and for answer they rowed on.
Until Gagne chose his mooring
"As if the chart were given"—
And may have been, for the first grapnel struck, held, and
the winch
Wound up the catch:
First of what would be seven
Pieces, sticky, green and hard . . .

. . . *Which in the tayl bears a sting*
Hard as any horn, and all
The body over
Set with spines, so that being alive still, it is not handled
Without danger. Whose aspect
Is very fierce and grim, for
Whenever they move, their eyes give a sound from their
eyelids
Much like unto
The tinkling of Brasse. Their age
Could never yet be surely

Known, but it is conjectured
They live long, and in great health
Flourish amayne
Like to all other Serpents, and therefore they grow so great.
Among the manifold kinds
As well known as unknown, this
Is by Pliny called the Dragon of Ocean, which haunteth
The deepest part
Only of the sea, showing
Now and then upon the Coasts

Of Norway, an hundred feet
Long and more, very hurtfull
And dangerous
To the Sea-men in calms and still weather, for they lift up
Themselves above the hatches
And suddenly catch a man
In their mouths, and so draw him out of the ship to his death.
And many times
They overthrow in the sea
A laden vessel with all

The wares therein contayned. And
Sometimes also they set up
So huge a coyl
Above the water that a moderate Bark (without sayls)
May passe through the same. Yet when
Grown to such great proportion
Whereby it doth harm to all Creation, the winds or clouds
Will take it up
Suddenly into the ayre,
And thereby a violent

Agitacion, shake the body
To pieces: parcels whereof
Mangled and torn

Asunder, have often been found, even in the tops of waves
        And floating at the surface . . .
    . . . The fog has closed in, for good
It would seem, and the sea is still as calm as if it had
        Yielded nothing
      Or, having relinquished, had
      Nothing—nothing more to yield.

      Gagne, as his name would imply,
      Wants a profit. "A monster,"
        He said last week,
"Is something shown. For money." Tourists visited the town
        To see the "skeleton" parts
      Before Gagne bundled his find
In cellophane and placed it in a plywood box filled with
        Formaldehyde.
      Offers have come in (one from Loch Ness)
      But Gagne has not yet set a price.

Richard Howard

Richard Howard was born and educated in Cleveland, Ohio, and studied at Columbia University and the Sorbonne. He is a distinguished translator from the French, and a critic of great versatility. His three earlier books of poems are *Quantities* (1962), *The Damages* (1967), and *Untitled Subjects* (1969) for which he was awarded the Pulitzer Prize for 1970. He is also the author of a monumental critical study, *Alone With America: Essays on the Art of Poetry in the United States since 1950*, which includes comprehensive studies of 41 contemporary American poets.